Elias Nason

A brief Record of Events in Exeter, N.H. during the Year 1861

Together with the Names of the Soldiers of this Town in the War

Elias Nason

A brief Record of Events in Exeter, N.H. during the Year 1861
Together with the Names of the Soldiers of this Town in the War

ISBN/EAN: 9783337307141

Printed in Europe, USA, Canada, Australia, Japan

Cover: Foto ©ninafisch / pixelio.de

More available books at **www.hansebooks.com**

A

BRIEF RECORD

OF

EVENTS IN EXETER, N. H.

DURING THE YEAR

1861,

TOGETHER WITH THE NAMES OF THE

SOLDIERS

OF THIS TOWN IN THE

WAR.

By Rev. ELIAS NASON.

Omnes eodem cogimur.—Hor.

EXETER:

PRINTED BY SAMUEL HALL.

1862.

ADVERTISEMENT.

As the year 1861 will be ever memorable on account of the most stupendous and wicked rebellion the world has ever known; and as every correct history of the country must derive its sources in a measure from the current events of the individual towns which go to make up the country, I have thought proper to select from my Daily Journal a few brief memoranda relating to Exeter, and to embody them; together with the names of our gallant soldiers; in this little brochure which I take the liberty to present as a New Year's Offering to our patriotic and worthy citizens.

[N. B. Meteorological observations were taken for the Smithsonian Institute at 7 A. M. and at 2 and 9 P. M. Only the maximum and minimum of the Barometer and Thermometer for each month are given.]

A BRIEF RECORD OF EVENTS

IN

EXETER 1861.

THE town of Exeter was settled by the Rev. John Wheelwright and others in 1638, and now contains 3269 inhabitants. Lat. 42.58 N. long. 70.55 W., time W. 4 h. 43 m. 40 s. distance from Washington 474 miles.

JANUARY, 1861.

1. Cloudy morning; but the sun soon shows itself and "Happy new year!" is ringing from every lip.
3. Severe snow storm during the day.—4. National fast.
4. Mr. H. P. Flower and A. M. Bryant married.
5. Mr Moses H. Stickney and Miss Harriet N. Barker married. Also Mr. John Codman and Miss Nancy White.
8. S. J. Court in session. Severe snow storm. Trees beautifully tinged with golden hues at sunset.
9. Mrs. Elizabeth Ann, wife of Thos. E. Fifield dies, aged 44 1-3 years.
10. High winds last night.—11. Fair, but very cold.
12. Mr. Eugene Thurston and Lydia E. Jones married.
13. Tlier.—17. at 7 A. M. and very cold through the day.
14. Mr. Reuben Swain dies aged 73.
15. Mrs. Sally Marden dies, aged 89. Dr. George W. Dearborn's store robbed of watches, jewelry, &c., to the amount of $115.
19. Bar. 30.80 at 7 A. M. Ther. 31. at 2. P. M.
21. Trees overladen with snow and ice. Scenery beautiful Rev. Mr. Taylor lectures on London.
23. Mr. Alvan White, powder manufacturer, dies, aged 59.
28. The celebrated Farmer will case now before the court.
29. Benj. M. Colby, Esq. and Miss Elizabeth D. Robinson married.

FEBRUARY—

1. Opens beautifully; cloudy in P. M.; snows at night.
3. Mr. Joseph Janvrin and Mrs. Anna B. Davenport married.
4. Bar. 30.80 at 7 A. M.

FEBRUARY, 1861.

7. Bar. 29.10 at 2 P. M.   A sudden snow tempest about 3 P. M. Sun sets clear.

8. Ther.—24. at 7 A. M.   Wind W. and sky clear. Average temperature of the day—17 1-3.

11. Ther. 54. at 2 P. M.—13. Beautifully clear morning.

15. Rain all day, with thunder and lightning about 6 P. M.

16. Weather clear and beautiful.

17. Lucian B. Robie dies, aged 57 1-2 years.

18. Students in the Academy contribute nearly $70 in aid of sufferers by famine in Kansas.

19. Bar. 30.80 at 7 A. M.—20. Snow and rain.

21. Trees covered with snow and ice; W. S. Abbott, Esq. delivers a lecture on "Education" at the Town Hall. Barn of Mr. J. J. Wiggin, destroyed by fire about 11 P. M.

22. Mr. Samuel Hatch, of Cass street, dies aged 86. A large and beautiful paraselene at 9 P. M.

23. Mrs. Mary Hatch, wife of the preceding, dies, aged 83 years 11 months.   They had lived together 64 years.

25. Trees sparkling with crystals.

27. Beautiful Aurora Borealis at 7 P. M.   House of Col. Robert Means much injured by fire.

MARCH—

1. Rains.

2. High School examined and appears well.   The bluebird [*amphelis sialis*] is heard.   Mrs. Abby P. Porter dies, aged 43.   Infant daughter of J. Atherton dies aged 2 yrs.

3. Ther. 63. at 2 P. M.   Mr. G. C. Tuttle and S. Cutts m.

4. Bells rung and National salute fired for the inauguration of Abraham Lincoln as President of the United States.

5. Magnificent golden clouds at sunset.   Francis O. French, Esq. and Miss Ellen Tuck married.

6. Mrs. Miriam D. James dies suddenly aged 40.

8. Ther. 1. at 7 A. M.   Bar. 30.50 at 7 P. M.   Wind N. W. Clear.   Leverett Saltonstall, lectures in the Town Hall on the Questions of the day.—10. Bar. 29.20 at 7 P. M.

12. Annual Election.   W. B. Morrill, Esq., Mod'r.   Nath'l Shute, Joseph D. Wadleigh and Josiah J. Folsom chosen Selectmen.   William H. Belknap, Town Clerk.   397 votes are cast for Berry and 182 for Stark.   J. Conner, Moses N. Collins & C. Burley are elected Representatives.

16. Snow about 9 inches deep and much drifted.   P. M. fair.

19. Annual examination of Phillips E. Academy which appears to be in a very prosperous condition.

21. Violent snow storm in the afternoon and through the night.

23. Bass (*labrax lineatus*) taken from the river in large quantities.—24. Pleasant.

26. Robins and bluebirds singing freely.

MARCH, 1861.

27. A bass weighing 27 lbs. is taken from the river. Rockingham Co. Bible Society, formed. Gov. I. Goodwin Pres't.

28. A splendid sunrise. Find a dandelion (*leontodon taraxacum*) in blossom on the margin of the river below the falls. An elegant Bible is presented to the " Star of the East" Lodge of Masons. Wm. B. Morrill, Esq. is appointed Post Master vice Daniel Melcher, Esq. Mr. Jas. Roach and Ann Hughes m.

APRIL—

1. Bar. 30.51 at 7 A. M. A flock of wild geese flies southward. Cloudy.—2. Furious snow storm all day.

3. Ther. 18. at 9 P. M.

4. James Dwight Nason dies, aged 20 years 5 months.

7. Mrs. Ruth Purinton dies, aged 70.

8. Schools in District No. 1 commence their session. The " Dido " arrives. A boy named McNamara is severely injured by the elevator in the factory.

9. S. J. Court sits, Judge Bellows presiding.

10. Mr. Richard Dow dies, aged 77. The blackbird (*T. merula*) appears. Mr. M. S. Holmes and C. Kimball m.

11. Fast day. Services in the churches. Splendid Aurora Borealis at 9 1-2 P. M.

12. Earth worms make their appearance.

13. Mr. E. O. Randall and C. Kelly m.

15. The elm is in blossom and frogs are heard.

16. Rain and snow.

17. Bar. 29.00 at 2 P. M. Wind W. stormy weather.

18. The Trailing Arbutus (*Epigœa repens*) appears in bloom.

19. Great excitement in town in reference to the attack on Fort Sumter. Mr. P. Broderick and C. Curtin m.

20. Academy students hoist a flag and fire 32 guns. " DUCIT AMOR PATRIAE."

22. A grand mass meeting, in respect to the war, at the Town Hall, Hon. C. H. Bell, presiding. Many Patriotic speeches made and money pledged for the support of soldiers.

23. Infant child of N. Swasey, Jr. dies. Ther. 66. at 2 P. M.

24. The Granite State Bank tender a loan of $20,000 to the State of N. H. for military purposes. Rockingham Co. Agr'l Soc. decide not to hold a Fair the ensuing autumn. Ladies of Exeter meet at Town Hall to make clothing for the soldiers. They form a Society and choose Mrs. E. S. Cobbs president. Rev. Mr. Lanphear repeats his sermon on the war at the Town Hall.

26. Jefferson Davis hung in effigy. *Houstonia cerulea* in bloom.

28. Mr. E. J. Conner catches in his wier two fine shad, the first of the season. Rain storm.

MAY, 1861.

1. Fair May Day.—A few flowers in bloom.
3. Mr. John H. Thing ploughs up a silver lever watch in good state of preservation after a burial of 9 years.
4. Ther. 29. at 9 P. M.
5. James E. C. Sawyer of the Academy departs for the war.
9. Swallows appear. Voted in a legal Town Meeting to raise a sum not over $5,000 for the benefit of soldiers and their families. Mr. Loring Newton and Miss Almeda Kimball married.
10. Mrs. Almira B. Prescott dies, aged 38. A beautiful para-helion at 5 P. M.
12. Fifty men or so are now drilling under Chas. H. Bell, Esq.
13. Citizens meet to form a "Home Guard," and choose Gen'l Andrew Chase as drill officer. Mr. James Folsom dies, aged 75 yrs. 5 1-2 mos.
15. Currants and strawberries in bloom. The 2d Maine Regt. passes through town. A large company assemble at the depot and a salute is fired.
16. The bobolink (*D. orizyvorus*) is heard. The Exeter Cornet Band give an excellent Concert at the Town Hall.
18. Mr. John M. Mallon, volunteer, and Miss Mary J. Smith married.
19. Minnie M. Fifield dies, aged 3 yrs. 7 mos. Rev. Mr. Nason preaches a sermon to the Volunteers on Psalm 20 : 5.
21. Mr. Samuel Caban dies suddenly, aged 61 yrs. 4 mos. The whippoor-will (*C. vociferus*) is heard.
23. Bar. 30.30 at 9 P. M.
25. Ladies present many articles of clothing to our volunteers, who leave for Portsmouth, attended by the Band, to join 2d N. H. Regt.—27. Bar. 29.20 at 2 P. M. Rain storm.
28. Appletree in bloom. Plum and cherry trees do not blossom at all.
30. Mr. Dennis Cokely's house and barn burned. Insured $350. It rained fourteen times in May.

JUNE—

1. Beautiful morning; and very warm day. Com. J. C. Long raises a spendid flag.
2. Bar. 30.27 at 9 P. M., and wind E. Cloudy. Rev. Charles Newhall becomes Pastor of the Elm St. Church. Mr. George G. Taylor dies, aged 22.
3. Hon. Gilman Marston enters on his duties as Col. of the 2d N. H. Regiment.
6. Ther. 50. at 7 A. M. Rain storm. Frank E. Bachelder dies, aged 6 years.
7. Maine 3d Regt passes through town and receives a collation from our citizens. The Academy Cadets drill under command of Mr. Dubois and make a fine appearance.

JUNE, 1861.

10. Citizens present a sword and other equipments to Col. G. Marston.

11. Rockingham Co. Conf. of churches meet here. Willie Senior dies, aged 8 yrs. The R. Co. Temp. Soc. meets. Exeter Cornet Band serenade the citizens in the evening. A new Catalogue of the Town Library is published. No. of Vols. about 3000.

13. Albert Andrews dies, aged 46. Beautiful Aurora Borealis at 9 P. M.

14. Members of H. School present Bible, pistol, etc. to Charles F. Smith, leaving for the war. Equipments are also presented to Lieut. W. H. Smith.

17. U. S. Dist. Court sits, Judge Harvey presiding.

18. S. J. Court sits. Justice S. D. Bell presiding. Lieut. Wm. H. Smith and Miss Susie Littlefield married.

20. Mr. Joel Lane dies, aged 69 yrs. 10 mos. Many citizens visit Boston to witness the departure of the 2d N. H. Regt.

21. Mr. G. H. Rundlett and Mrs. E. A. Robinson married.

22. A gold watch and clothes are stolen from Messrs. Carpenter & Irons while bathing. Mr. Nason delivers a lecture on "National Music." at the Town Hall, the band attending and performing our national airs.

23. A storehouse of the Exeter Man'g Co. burned at 10 P. M.

25. Morris Bros., Pell & Trowbridge give a concert at T. Hall.

26. A Maine Regt. receives a collation from our citizens at the depot. Mr. Theophilus Smith dies aged 80. Luella, infant child of Mr. J. Weeks, dies. Bar. 29.20 at 2 P. M. Wind S. West.

27. Steamboat "Clipper" arrives.

29. Mr. Alfred C. Smith, printer, dies, aged 24. Schools in Districts 1 and 2 close.

JULY—

1. A very brilliant comet seen at 9 P. M., tail about 90 deg. long. Fair weather from June 8th to July 2d.

2. Ther. 57 at 7 P. M. A refreshing rain falls. Mr. J. M. Head's child buried. Miss C. A. Jacobs gives readings in poetry, &c.

3. Strawberries are plentiful: but no plums or cherries here, or elsewhere in the vicinity.

4. Fair and warm. Gunpowder freely expended. Sab. School of the 1st Cong. Soc'y celebrate the day with speeches, music, &c., in the grove near the depot. The Elm St. Baptist Soc. also have a pleasant picnic by the river.

7. Elder Edwin Burnham preaches at the Town Hall. Comet very brilliant in Ursa Major.

8. Ther. 92 at 2 P. M. Fair. Wind West.

JULY, 1861.

9. Examination of the Academy and some thirty students leave for college. Sudden thunder gust at 5 P. M.
10. Probate Court sits. The pupils of Miss Bell's School contribute $14. to the Ladies' Aid Soc. Beach parties numerous. Mr. Timothy Wentworth and Miss Adelia A. Sibley married.
11. Comet moving south. *Pyrola uniflora* (rare) in bloom. beautiful thunder clouds at sunset--rays extending 50deg. in all directions.
12. Miss Hannah Colcord dies, aged 84. Infant child of Mr. Geo. Ellison dies, 6 mos. old.
14. Bar. 30.15 at 7 A. M. Cloudy and rain. Mr. Wm. G. Cate and Miss Data J. Lang married.
18. Business is remarkably dull. Carriage and cotton manufacturing have nearly ceased.
20. Bar. 29.60 at 2 P. M. Wind S. W. Mrs. Mary York dies, aged 73 yrs. Showers in P. M. Mr. John E. Wilbur opens a recruiting office at the Town Hall. Schooner " Northern Warrior," Capt. Kent arrives.
21. Fair. Col. G. Marston wounded in the right arm at the battle of " Bull Run." Wm. H. Morrill also wounded in the hand. F. L. Tebbetts taken prisoner.
22. Great excitement on account of the recent battle in which a number of our soldiers were engaged. A clear day—most of the ministers and teachers absent.
27. Remarkably beautiful and quiet day. General topic of conversation—WAR !
27, Rains in A. M. Thunder and lightning at night.
30. A daughter of Mr Rock dies aged 8 years. The old board of officers of the E. Manuf'g Co. re-elected.

AUGUST—

1. Party of 16 Exeter boys encamp at Hampton Beach. The " army worm " in great numbers appears suddenly in Mr. Gilman's field. Very little secession sentiment in Exeter.
3. Ther. 86. at 2. P. M. Fair and wind west.
4. Ella Adams dies suddenly, aged 14.
5. A great war meeting at the Town Hall. An account of the battle of " Bull Run " given.
7. Town vote to pay a sum not exceeding $15 per week to the families of soldiers enlisted.
8. Mrs. Margaret Mason dies, aged 46. Capt. Wilbur's Company leave for Concord, to join N. H. 3d Regt. A Gas company organized and stock taken.
9. Mr. Jesse Robinson dies, aged 72 yrs. 5 mos.
10. Bar. 29.70 at 9 P. M. Showery. Blue berries abundant — 8 cts. per qt.

AUGUST, 1861.

12. Ther. 53. at 9 P. M.   Fair.   Schools in District No. 1, commence.

13. Heavy rain all day.

14. Ditto. R. Mu. Fire Ins. Co. meet and choose Directors.

15. Col. G. Marston, suffering from his wound, returns to town. Great fears for the safety of Washington.

18. Elder Burnham preaches in T. Hall. Beautiful Cirrus clouds in the P. M. Mr. Chas. H. Folsom and Miss Mary A. Sutton married.

19. Schools Dist. No. 1 & 2, commence.

21. The lads of the High School and their teachers visit Hampton Beach. Bar. 30.35 at 7 P. M. Fair. Mr. Gilman Barker has 15 sheep killed by a dog about this time.

22. Messrs. Conners' Fish and Meat market entered by burglars. Mr. Benj. Swain appointed Police officer, vice, J. A. Fogg. Mr. R. Carter is recruit'g for the 4th Regt.

23. Maine 7th Reg. passes through town for the seat of war in fifteen passenger cars. Soldiers of Co. D return from Concord on a furlough.

24. The "army worm" disappears. Mr. T. Moses in his 95th year visits the town.

26. Rev. N. Hooper is called to the 1st Baptist church.

27. Miss Ellen Fellowes dies, aged 19 1-2 years. A boy 4 or 5 yrs. old, has his arm broken by the cars. Patrick Gilroy takes a turtle near the Ox-bow, weighing 26 lbs ; 13 inches long. Rev. Dr. Hitchcock visits this town.

30. Southern corn is selling at $1 25 per bag.

31. Fair; and so the weather has been since the 22d. L. cardinalis, Indian pipe (monotropa) etc. in bloom.

SEPTEMBER—

1. Mr. J. B. Wadleigh, late conductor on the B. & M. R. R. dies, aged 47 1-2 yrs. Mr. John Marsh and wife are burned to death.

3. B. W. Cram and James Jack escape from jail. The former is retaken. N. K. Leavitt, Esq., is appointed Jail-keeper, vice John S. Brown, Esq., resigned.

9. There are now 110 Students at the Academy.

7. Armenia C. Stacy dies, aged 12 1-3 yrs. Charming day.

11. A refreshing rain occurs after a long drouth. Mr. Peter Leighton digs up a thimble in the rear of "Squamscott House," marked 1772.

13. Lovely moonlight evening. Many social parties in town at this season.—15. Ther. 79 1-2. at 2 P. M. Fair.

18. Miss Abigail Parks dies, aged 73.

20. John E. Lyford dies aged 10 mos. Fruit of every kind very scarce. Corn and potato harvest abundant.

2

SEPTEMBER, 1861.

22. Sch'r " Caroline " arrives with gaspipe from Philadelphia. Coal is selling at $6.50 per ton. Rainy day.

23. Mr. Lewis Mitchell dies suddenly, aged about 60. Ladies meet for supplying clothing to the soldiers.

24. Wm. N. Tilton dies aged 48. N. Swasey, Jr. dies, aged 30 yrs 5 mos. Maine 9th Reg. Col. Rich, passes through town.

25. Ther. 47. at 7 P. M. Fair.

26. Edward Bachelder wounded in the arm by premature discharge of a gun. National Fast. Well observed, most of the stores closed and service in the churches. Mr. J. Swasey badly kicked in the face by a horse.

28. Bar. 29.51 at 7 A.M. Fair Wind west. Mrs. Hannah P. Fogg dies aged 75. Mr. Edward C. Towle and Mary J. Vaudusee married at or near this date.

29. The churches take up a contribution for the hospitals at Washington; in all about $90. Capt. Edw. Ludington is recruiting at the Squamscott House for U. S. A.

30. Bar. 30.50 at 2. P. M. Fair. Mr. D. W. Downes begins a Singing School. Mr. N. Loud's house entered by burglars. Ladies of Hampton send $3.65 to Exeter ladies for the soldiers.

OCTOBER—

1. Horace E. Pitman dies, aged 2 years 22 days. A pleasant tea party at the Town Hall, for benefit of the hospitals at Washington. About $210 realized.

2. Ther. 69. at 2 P. M. Fair.

3. N. A. Shute, Esq. and Miss Ellen M. Holbrook married.

4. A circus in town. Not largely patronized.

5. Rainy day. Col. Marston leaves for Washington.

6. Mr. Jeremiah Sanborn dies, aged 71.

8. U. S. D. Court sits, Judge Harvey presiding.

9. Beautiful P. M. Yarrow, St. Johnswort, (*H. perforatum*) red clover, etc. still in bloom.

10. Leaves of the maple beautifully tinted—some of a pale golden hue with rich crimson edges : why ?—11. Rain storm.

14. Mrs. Ann Elizabeth Blake dies, aged 26 yrs. 9 mos. Ripe raspberries and strawberries gathered from Mr. N. Week's garden. The Gas Co. are laying down pipes for the gas ; about fifty men employed.

17. Ladies send a large box of articles, blankets, bandages, books, etc., etc., to the Hospital at Washington.

18. An alarm of fire at night from an old house below the factory. Mr. D. W. Stevens holds a cattle market near Mr. Mc. Duffie's.

19. Rain. The Peake Family Bell Ringers give a Concert at Town Hall.

OCTOBER, 1861.

21. The first frost of the season occurred last night. Battle at Ball's Bluff. Valentine A. Pickering killed.

22. Heavy frost last night.

24. Dr. F. P. Cummings appointed assistant Surgeon in the Navy. Lieut. O. M. Head and Capt. II. H. Pearson are raising recruits.

25. Bar. 30.59 at 7 A. M., fair. Schooner "Thomas Page" is taking in 200 cords of wood for Philadelphia.

25. N. A. Shute, Esq., is appointed agent to receive subscriptions to the National Loan. Ther. 21. at 7 A. M. Ice made nearly an inch in thickness last night.

29. Mr. Geo. II. Reynolds and Miss Ann A. Anderson married.

30. Bar. 29.45 at 9 P. M., pleasant. Ladies have sent 25 India rubber blankets etc. to our soldiers of the 2d Regiment.

NOVEMBER—

1. Bar. 30.35 at 9 P. M. Fair.

3. Severe S. E. snow storm last night and to day. Highest tide in the river since 1816. Great anxiety in respect to the Naval Expedition. N. H. 3d and 4th Regt. in it.

4. Sun rises in a cloudless sky; air soft and balmy—" O Nature! how in every charm supreme!"

5. Master Walter Dearborn buried. Ther. 56. at 2 P. M.

6. A large flock of robins observed. Probate Court in session—Judge Stickney presiding.

7. Naval action and Union victory at Port Royal witnessed by many of our soldiers on board the " Atlantic."

9. Stormy.

10. Three females baptized in the river just above the "Great Bridge." Sunset extremely fine. Aster and golden rod still in bloom.

12. Miss Emily F. Greenleaf dies, aged 19 yrs. 7 mos. 14 days. Mrs. Mary Kennedy dies, aged about 88. Mary Ellen Quin dies, aged 18 yrs. The Hutchinson Family give a concert at the T. Hall. Mr. Sam'l Palmer raises a parsnip 25 inches in cir. and weighing 3 lbs. 10 oz. High winds. Walnuts plentiful.

13. Rev. N. Hooper is settled over the 1st Baptist Church.

14. Bright and beautiful morning. Ladies—each with a billet of wood for fuel—meet at Concert Hall to knit and sew for the soldiers. One of them has knit 12 prs. stockings for them with her own hands. Mr. Geo. F. Richmond and Miss Narcissa D. Nelson, married; also Mr. Joel A. Leighton and Mrs. Elizabeth H. Broughton.

15. A few flakes of snow, first of the season, fall in A. M.

16. Schools in Dist. No. 1. close. Calvin L. Dearborn of Co. L, N. H. 2d Regt. dies of typhoid fever at Washington.

NOVEMBER, 1861.

17. Ther. 22 at 7 A. M.   Fair.   Anniversary of the Mission
    S. School.   Addresses by Messrs. Nason and Lanphear.

19. Quarterly examination I of Phillips Academy.   Seventy
    students have not been tardy during the term.   J. L.
    Sibley, Esq., gives the Academy $100 in addition to the
    "Sibley Fund," for purchasing books for indigent stu-
    dents.   Mrs Judith W. Colcord dies, aged 76.

22. Capt. H. H. Pearson's company leave to join the 6th Regt.,
    Col. Mack, at Keene.

23. Cold and misty morning.   Rain.

24. Bar. 29. 40 at 7 P. M.   Pleasant.   Mr. Geo. W. Stevens
    and Rosa A. Sargent, married about this time.

25. Snow falls to the depth of four or five inches, and merry
    sleigh bells announce the advent of the winter season.

27. Poultry selling at 12 to 14 cts.—supply abundant.

28. ANNUAL THANKSGIVING.   Fair and quite dry.   Church-
    es open and well filled.   Co. B, 3d Regt., mostly from
    Exeter, dine on turkies and sweet potatoes at Hilton
    Head, S. C.

29. Dull and drizzling day.   Our citizens generally disposed to
    sustain the policy of the President.   Mr. Jno. Leavitt,
    Jr., and Irene S. Dolloff married about this time.

DECEMBER.

Dec. 1. Cloudy morning and rain in P. M.

  2. Opens fair and cold.   Skating now enlivens the day.

  3. Miss Dolly Rundlett dies, aged about 82.

  5. Sam'l Greenleaf dies, aged 11 yrs.

  6. Snow.   Miss Marry E. Tilton dies, aged 37.   Sword pre-
     sented to Capt. H. H. Pearson.   Bar. 30.65. 2 P. M.

  8. Ther. 55 at 2 P. M.   Clear—wind west.

  9. Fine day.   Robert A. Cross buried from the 1st Cong.
     Church, aged about 40.   Schools in Dist. No. 1. commence.

10. Warm for the season.

12. Fair.   Ladies continue busily at work for the soldiers; they
    have recently sent to N. H. 2d Reg't, 120 prs. socks, 30
    prs. mittens, 12 prs. wristers, etc. etc.—also one box by
    Dr. Howe to Missouri, containing 50 prs. socks, etc.   They
    have, moreover, made 175 prs. shirts and drawers for
    Concord.

15. Warm.   Maple buds are nearly bursting and a dandelion
    is found in bloom.

16. Col. Marston is dangerously wounded by the accidental dis-
    charge of a pistol in the hands of a boy of Lt. Col. Fiske.

17. Charming day.

20. Michael Murphy and Mary Brodrick married near this
    date.   Many trophies, caps, fans, cotton, etc. received
    from our soldiers at Hilton Head.

DECEMBER, 1861.

21. Very cold day. The gas works are completed and the town lighted.

23. Bar. 20.02 at 9 P. M. A blustering snow storm—wind N. E.

.24. Ladies send a large box containing 9 quilts, 3 blankets, 44 new and many old pillow cases, shirts, bandages, etc. etc, to the "Sanitary Commission" at Washington. Ladies of the 2d Parish held a Levee at the Town Hall. Trees covered with crystals. Funeral of Calvin L. Dearborn, brought from Washington, at the lower church.

.25. CHRISTMAS. Santa Claus, well filled stockings and Christmas Trees present their annual store of "good things" to the children. Mr. Joseph T. Porter and Miss Ann M. Wiggin, married. The Unitarian S. School have a very pleasant meeting at the house of Chas. Burley, Esq.

.26. Ther. 8. at 7 A. M.—clear and cold—fine sleighing. Mrs. Eliza Barlow, dies, aged 35. Our soldiers from the 8th Regt. at home on furlough. The material of their clothing is wretched stuff indeed! Whose fault?

.27. Dull, rainy morning—Fair in P. M., wind high through the night. One family has knit 20 pairs of stockings for the soldiers.

28. A tempestuous morning. About 100 students now at the Academy and 63 at the H. School.

29. Mr. John P. Leavitt dies, aged 64. Rev. Mr. Bird gives an interesting lecture on Syria.

30. Mrs. Martha Smith dies, aged 69.

31. Sun rises in a cloudless sky—partially eclipsed. At 5 min. past 9 the obscuration passes away and the day continues and closes mild and beautiful.

So terminates the fleeting and eventful year! Year of treason ; year of lofty patriotism ; year of battle, agony, death ; of progress, liberty ; year of tearful sowing for a golden harvest ; year of God's great mercy.

"Eheu! fugaces, Posthume, Posthume, Labuntur anni ;" sadly moans the Venusian bard ; but under clearer light shall we not with a hero of his day, exclaim, "Forgetting those things which are behind and reaching forth unto those things which are before, I press toward the mark for the prize of the high calling of God in Christ Jesus."

Names of Exeter Soldiers Enlisted in 1861.

Abbott, Sewell A. 8th Regt. Co. B.

Bennett, Chas. 8th Reg. Me.

Bennett, Edw'd T. 6th Regt. Co. C.

Bennett, Jno. H. 2d Regt. Co. E.

Berry, Woolbury 3d " Co. B.

Bowley, Albert 6th " " C.

Bowley, Benj. F. " " "

Brigham, Asa P. 11th " Mass Musician.

Brigham, Geo. H. " " "

Brigham, Bruce " " "

Brigham, Ephraim " " "

Brown, Geo. 14th Regt. Mass.

Bryant, Jno. S. Corp. 3d Regt. Co. B.

Caban, Sam'l 3d Regt. Co. B.

Carlisle, James " " "

Carver, E. " " "

Carter, Gideon Jr. " "

Chase, James 2d Regt. Co. E.

Clark, Geo. W. Serg't 14th Regt. Mass. Co. E.

Clark, Wm. A. Corp. 12th Regt. Mass.

Clement, J. W. 3d Regt. Co. B.

Coakley, Timothy 8th Regt. Co. B.

Colcord, Wm. H. 2d " Co. E.

Colcord, Chas. E. " " " discharged.

Conner, Freeman Capt. 44th Regt. Co. D, N. Y.

Conner, Edw'd J. Capt. 17th Regt. U. S. A.

Colbath, Warren 3d Regt. Co. B.

Cobbs, Geo. S. Serg't 8th " " B.

Clough, Geo. 3d Regt. Co. B.

Clough, Tho. H. 6th Regt. Co. C.

Clough, Ezekiel " " "

Corcoran, Frank " " "

Cummings, Dr. E. P. Ass't Surg. " Roebuck."

Currier, Andrew J. 2d Regt. Co. E.

Curtis, A. O. 13th Regt. Mass.

Davis, A. J. 6th Regt. Co. C.

Dearborn, Calvin L. 2d Reg. Co. E. died, Nov. 13.

Dearborn, A. 3d Reg. Co. B.

Dearborn, W. 3d " "

Dearborn, J. S. Cook's battery Mass.

Dodge, J. E. 22d Reg. Co. B, Mass. Hall's Hill, Va.

Donnavan, Cornelius 3d Regt. Co. B, Mass.

Donnavan, J. 8th Regt. Co. B.

Doody, J 6th Regt. Co. C.

Doody, W. " " "

Dudley, S. G. 3d " " B.

Dudley, D. W. " " B.

Durgin, D. W. Corp. 8th Regt. Co. B.

Dyer, J. Jr. 8th Regt. Co. B.

Dewhurst, G. W.—Act. master, Navy.

Elkins, J. 6th Regt. Co. C.

Elliott, Dan'l W. 3d Regt. Co.

Ellison, Horace. Mass. dis.

Farnham, Jno.

Finn, Jno. 3d Regt. Co. B.

Floyd, C. W. 2d Regt. Co. E.

Floyd, Sam'l " "

Fogg, Andrew J. 2d Lt. 3d Regt. Co. B.

Folsom, C. E. 17 Regt. Mass.

Greenleaf, Matthew A. Ord'ly Serg., 3d Regt. Co. E.

15

Giddings, Geo. H. Corp. 3d Regt. Co. B.

Gill, Isaiah W. Acting master, Navy.

Goodwin, Sewell in the Navy.

Gordon, John 25th Regt. Mass. now at Annapolis.

Gill, Nath'l 11th Regt. Mass., musician.

Hale, Jno. 2d Regt. Co. E., now with Capt. Gill.

Hale, Chas. E. fifer, 8th Regt. Co. B.

Haley, Ira, 8th Regt. Co. B.

Hall, Horace J. " "

Hall, Edw'd F. " "

Haines, Isaiah F. 2d Regt. Co. E.

Haines, Daniel D. Corp. 8th, Regt. Co. B.

Hartnett, Dan'l P. 8th Regt., Co. B.

Hartnett, Thos. 6th Regt. Co. C.

Hartnett, Michael. Navy.

Hartnett, J. H. 2d Regt. Co. E.

Head, O. M. Adg't 8th Regt.

Head, J. N. Serg. 2d Regt. Co. C.

Hodgdon, S. S. 6th " " C.

Huse, J. H. 2d " " E.

Hibberd, E. W, 3d " Clerk.

James, G. R. 3d " Co. D.

Janvrin, G. N. Cobb's battery.

Janvrin, J. E. Ast. Surg. 2d Regt.

Julian, G. A. Cobb's batt. Mass

Keefe, Wm. 6th Regt. Co. C.

Kelley, D. G. 8th " " B.

Kimball, G. A. in the Navy.

Lamprey, S. Corp. 3d Regt. Co. B.

Leavitt, E. A. 2d Regt. Co. E.

Leavitt, C. H. 4th " Mass.

Leavitt, J. W. 3d " Co. B.

Leavitt, A. J. " Mass.

Leighton, J. A. Serg. 6th Regt. Co. C.

Lovering, E. 6th Regt. Co. C.

Manjoy, J. in the Navy.

Marston, G. Col. 2d Regt.

Marston, W. S. 3d Regt. Co B.

Marsh, A. F. 6th " " C.

McNary T. fifer, 3d " " in a Manchester Co.

McNeal, D. F. 19th Regt. Mass.

Melvin, M. 8th, " Co. B.

Morrill, W. H 2d " Co. E.

Murphy, J. 8th " " B.

Merrill, A. 12th Regt. Mass. Co. E.

Murphy, D. 2d Regt. Co. E.

Nason, P. F. clerk, 22d Mass. Regt. at Hall's Hill, Va.

Nealey, B. in the Navy.

Payson, T. K. drum major, 24th Regt. Mass.

Payson, J. C. commissary department, 13th, Regt. Mass.

Pearson, H. H. Capt. 6th Regt. Co. C.

Perkins, A. M. 2d. Lt., 2d Regt. Co. E.

Pike, D. 2d Regt. Co. E.

Pickering, V. A. 2d Regt. Mass. Killed at Ball Bluff.

Prescott, J. E. 3d Regt. Co. B.

Reardon, M. 6th Regt. Co. C.

Robinson, J. B. 6th " " "

Robinson, W. 2d " " E.

Rock, J. 6th Regt. Co. C.

Rowell, J. Sergt. 6th Regt. Co. C.

Ryan, W. 6th, Regt. Co. C.

Rundlett, F.—Navy.

Senior, W. 3d Regt. Co. B.

Smith, M. M. 6th Regt. Co. C.

Smith, G. H. " " " "

Smith, W. H. 1st Lt. 2d Regt. Co. E.

Smith, C. clerk. 2d Regt.

Smith, J. 3d Regt. Co. B.

Sleeper, W. H. 3d Regt. Co. B.

Stacy, —— Navy.

Stevens, G. W. 6th " " C.

Staples, —— Navy.

Stone, D. in the navy, " Roebuck."

Stone, J. D. 3d Regt. Co. B.

Stockman, F. 6th, " " C.

Sullivan J. jr. Medical Cadet, St. Louis.

Sullivan, P. W. 6th Regt. Co. C.

Swain, G. W. " " " "

Swasey, W. 12th Regt. Mass.

Taylor, G. A. 2d, Regt. Co. E.

Tanner, J. " " " "

Tebbetts, J. 8th " " B.

Thing, G. E. 8th " " B.

Thing, J. H 3d " " B.

Thing, G. H. 2d " " E.

Thurston, J. O. 2d " " E.

Twilight, W. H. " " " E. now 1st L. Artillery, Mass

Tebbetts, F.L. 2nd Regt. Co. E.

Tebbetts, J. P. "Macedonian."

Tebbetts, W. V. B. 17th Regt. Mass.

Veasey, W.G. Lt. Col. 3d Vt. Regt.

Watson, I. M. 1st Corp'l 3d Regt. Co. B.

Wainwright, W. in the Navy, " Kearsarge."

Warren, E. in the Navy.

Weeks, Josh. 6th Regt. Co. C.

Weeks, Jer. S. 3d " " B.

Weeks, N. in the Navy.

Weeks, H. 6th Regt. Co. C.

White, S. " " " "

Whitehouse W.

Wilbur, J. F. Capt. 6th Regt. Co. C.

Wyman, W. 4th Regt.

Willey J. 12th Regt. Mass. Co. E.

Willey, Alfred 3d Regt. Me.

Willey, H. " "

Young, J. R. 8th Regt, Co. B.

Young, C. W. " " " "

The 3d Regt. is at Camp Beaufort, Lower Potomac, Md.— The 4th at Hilton Head; the 5th at Annapolis, Md.; the 6th at Keene, and the 7th and 8th at Manchester.

RECORD OF EVENTS

IN

EXETER 1862.

A BRIEF RECORD

OF

EVENTS IN EXETER, N. H.

DURING THE YEAR

1862;

TOGETHER WITH THE NAMES OF THE

SOLDIERS

OF THIS TOWN IN THE

WAR.

BY REV. ELIAS NASON.

"——————Dum loquimur, fugerit invida
Ætas; carpe diem, quam minimum credula postero."--HOR.

EXETER:
FOGG AND FELLOWES,
PRINTED BY SAMUEL HALL.
1863.

ADVERTISEMENT.

TIME rolls its ceaseless course and brings us through many changes—sad and joyous—to the opening of another year. In the eventful and blood-stained year gone by, some of us have experienced " partings such as press the blood from out young hearts;"—some have followed " loved ones " to the house appointed for all the living;—some have met the foe in the stern conflict on the battlefield; some have nobly shed their blood in the defence of their native land. In *such* a year, the history of this single town alone would be the history of the nation; would fill ponderous volumes with events, romantic, tragical and momentous. Such history cannot be written; it lives however, in our memories, whose deep cells a " single word " may sometimes perchance unlock and bring the thrilling scenes again to view.

From my Daily Record of our busy life, I have therefore selected some " vestigia rerum," which; together with the names of our patriotic soldiers, who ever share our warmest sympathies and the salutations of the New Year, I would respectfully present to the loyal and liberty-loving citizens of Exeter.

☞ The observations in meteorology were made for the Smithsonian Institution and according to its rules, at 7 A. M. and 2 and 9 P. M. The maximum and minimum only of the barometer and thermometer for each month are given. When the name of a regiment is omitted, New Hampshire is understood.

A BRIEF RECORD OF EVENTS

IN

EXETER 1862.

Exeter, N. H., on the Boston and Maine Railroad, 49 miles
N. of Boston, is in N. Latitude 42, 58 ; and in W. Longitude,
70, 55. The central village is very beautifully situated at the
head of tidal water and of navigation on the Squamscot river ;
its dwelling houses are neat and commodious and its streets well
shaded with elm, maple, locust, fir and other ornamental trees.
It has eight, or nine, churches ; a court house of considerable
architectural beauty ; two hotels ; a well endowed academy and
several manufacturing establishments. Population 3269.

JANUARY, 1862.

1. Cold and windy. Hon. John Sullivan receives 76 votes in
   the State Convention for Governor. Hon. C. H. Bell is
   chosen a member of the State Central Committee for this
   county. Dr. Wm. G. Perry prepares his annual bill of the
   mortality of Exeter, from which it appears that the whole
   number of deaths in town in 1861, was 58 : of which 29
   were males and 29 females. Bar. 29.30 at 2 P. M

2. Last night very cold and tempestuous. Wind N. W.

3. Mr. Oliver Lane kills four hogs—weighing in all 2150 lbs.—
   fattened in one pen. Mrs. Sarah Ann, wife of Thomas
   McNary, fifer in the 3d N. H. regt. dies, aged 22 years.

5. A very cold and uncomfortable Sabbath. Wind N. W.—
   Ther. 1° at 7 A. M.

6. The pupils of the 2d District Grammar School, with their
   very excellent teacher, Mr. Aura L. Gerrish, enjoy a
   sleigh ride to Portsmouth and the Navy Yard. An alarm
   of fire at the house of Mr. George Smith, High st. Dam-
   age trifling.

7. Alva Wood, Esq. nominated candidate for the State Senate.
   Col. G. Marston, nearly recovered from his wound, is now
   in command of the gallant N. H. 2d reg't.

8. Very fine sleighing.—Many people skating on the river and
   Miss A. M. is said to lead the van. Four lads expelled

JANUARY, 1862.

    from the academy. Cause;—best known to themselves.—

- Henry B. Wells chosen State Committee for this county. Very splendid sunset.

9. Box of quilts, pillow cases, etc. sent to Capt. H. H. Pearson, Co. C. sixth N. H. reg't. at Washington, D. C., by the ladies of Exeter.

10. Thursday opens mildly and the sun shines out very pleasantly at 9 A. M. Many of our mechanics are employed in the Portsmouth Navy Yard. Ther. 42° at 2. P. M.

11. The wind blew very strong from the N. W. last night. Rev. Mr. Willey, Sec'y of the N. H. Bible Society in town.— Many skating on the river.

12: Dull and cloudy—raining hard at 6 P. M.

13. Beautiful interblending of cirrus, stratus and cumulus clouds, at 7 A. M. Mr. Daniel A. Shaw has one foot severely cut by an axe slipping accidentally from the hand of Mr. Edwin Dearborn.

14. Mr. George Carter and Miss Mary H. Haines are married. Rockingham State Convention assemble here. Also, Councillor Convention, District No. 1. Mr. Asa E. Perkins of this town, member of the N. Y. 40th—[Mozart] regt. dies in Fairfax Co. Va., of congestion of the brain. Bar. 30.63 at 7. A. M.

15. Trees gleaming beautifully in silver sheen.

17. Ther. 1° at 7. A. M.

18. The 6th N. H. regt.—which contains about 40 Exeter men, has arrived at Hatteras Island.

20. Mr. Ezekiel Hook dies, aged 81 years and 7 months. A N. E. snow storm, which began on Saturday, is still raging.— Yesterday the particles of snow were acuminate—to-day they are flocculent and then granular.

21. Wind N. E. all day—snow. Mr. Asa Perkins buried. Piscataqua Association meets at the Rev. Mr. Nason's church. Rev. Mr. Eldridge lectures on the social and religious condition of Georgia. S. J. Court sits—Judge S. D. Bell, presiding. Charles Smith aged 14 years skates from " Beach Hill " to the village—4 miles—in 30 minutes.

22. The storm continues through the day. Snow is now 12 inches deep. Mrs. Martha Lee dies aged 80 years and 11 mos. A box containing about 40 packages is sent by ladies to our soldiers at Hilton Head. S. C. Nimbus clouds at 2 P. M. for six successive days.

23. Mrs. Hannah Wiggin dies aged 87 years and 7 months.

24. Exeter Agricultural Library Association formed, Hon. John Sullivan President, John E. Gardner, Esq. Sec'y.

25. Snows and rains—a very disagreeable day indeed.

26. Snow is now about 20 inches deep. The Rev. Mr. Lanphear lectures before the " Christian Fraternity."

JANUARY, 1862.

27. The snow crust is sufficiently hard to sustain a man. Smelts are plentiful and selling at 6 cents per dozen.
28. Many of our ladies engaged in knitting for the soldiers. A splendid parahelion at 4 o'clock P. M. I count 40 persons skating below the "Falls."
29. It is snowing fast at 8 o'clock A. M. Ther. 17°. Wind N.
30. Mr. A. P. Wordsworth aged 63 years dies suddenly and his remains are carried to Hartford, Ct., for interment.
31. A clear and beautiful day. Fine sleighing. Albert F. Marsh, Co. C. N. H. 6th regt. dies at Camp Winfield, Hatteras Island, N. C., aged 18 years.

FEBRUARY—

2. A beautiful Sabbath. Churches well attended.
3. Streets well lighted by gas. Town healthful.
5. Dr. Gleason commences a course of very popular lectures at the town hall. Truth and error are amusingly interblended. 10. Beautiful corona solis at sunset.
11. Mr. Thos. E. Boutelle and Miss Abbie M. Head are married.
14. Mrs. Lucretia O., wife of the late Alex'r H. Everett, and daughter of Hon. O. Peabody dies in Boston—in her 76th year. Her remains brought to Exeter for interment.
17. Ther.—3° at 7. Bar. 30.50. Chas. H. Leavitt, of the Mass. 29th regt. in town on a furlough.
18. Bells are rung at noon and at 5 P. M., and 24 guns are fired in commemoration of the capture of Fort Donnelson by Gen. U. S. Grant. The Me. 12th regt. Col. Neal Dow, passes through town. Anniversary of the "Mission School," at the Town Hall in the evening. Mr. Wm. R. Leavitt, Co B, 3d N. H. regt. dies at Hilton Head, S. C. aged 51.
19. Ther. 43° at 2 P. M.
20. Trees delicately covered with light feathery snow.
21. Miss Susan F. Morrison, daughter of Mrs. Benning Marston dies, aged 24 1-2 years.
22. Washington's birth day is commemorated by a meeting of the citizens at the Town Hall, the reading of Washington's Farewell Address, etc.
23. Ther. 43. at 2 P. M. Mrs. Sarah Sherburne Rand dies, aged 86 3-4 years.
24. Bar. 29.05 at 9 P. M. Rain, thunder and lightning at 2 P. M. followed by a rainbow. Trees struck in the vicinity—weather very changeable through the day. Messrs. Head and Jewell have resumed the carriage manufacture.
25. Very cold and tempestuous last night. "Box" to Co.B 3 reg.
26. A beautifully clear day, save the appearance of a dun colored cloud, semilunar in form, and 40° high in the south at 2 P. M. 27. Mr. Haven Berry d. of consumption, aged 35 y.
28. It snows all day. Snow is now between three and four feet

February, 1862.

  deep in the forest. The children of the primary School District No. 2, make a quilt of 61 squares each having the name of a contributor for the N. H. 2d regt.

March—

1. This month opens fair and beautiful.
3. Ther. 5. at 7 A. M. Exhibition of Mr. E. S. French's school. The declamation, music, tableaux, etc., are all good. Mrs. Susan, wife of Mr. Oliver Lane dies, aged 26 years and 8 mos.
[4. Bar. 29.24 at 2 P. M. Many wells dry. While the barometer stands at this point, the smoke from the chimneys near the river is ascending perpendicularly—Why?
5. A morning union prayer meeting at the Lower Church at 8 o'clock,—to be held weekly. Winnie M. daughter of Mr. John M. and Mary J Mallon dies. Twenty-five pupils admitted to the High School.
6. Exhibition of the High School at the Town Hall, which is finely decorated and crowded with people. Exercises very interesting, especially the original, patriotic, dialogue.
7. Robins heard—" Sweet harbingers of spring." The winter has been dry and the town healthful.
9. The Rev. Mr. Nason lectures before the " Christian Fraternity." James H. Gasand, 14th Mass. regt. dies about this time at Fort Albany, near Washington, D. C. Battle between the " Monitor " and " Merrimack." Asa Beals, formerly of this town, aged 32, is killed on board the " Cumberand."
11. Blue birds are heard. Annual Town meeting. Wm. B. Morrill, Esq. Moderator. Votes thrown for governor—Berry, 364 ; Stark, 154 ; Wheeler, 9. Jos. D. Wadleigh, Josiah J. Folsom and A. J. Towle. Selectmen. W. H. Belknap, Town Clerk. Moses N. Collins, Jos. C. Hilliard and Abraham P. Blake. Representatives. A. J. Fogg, Register of Deeds. The N. H. 2d regt. present Col. G. Marston a sword worth $225.
12. Mrs. Lizzie B. (Holbrook) wife of Mr. Aura L. Gerrish, Teacher, dies, aged 25 years.
13. Bar. 30.33 at 9 P. M. Daniel Gilman Hatch, Esq. late of Covington, Ky., dies, aged 64. He was b. Aug. 3, 1798. Ossian E. Dodge gives a musical entertainment at the Town Hall.
15. A severe snow storm all day. J. N. Head, Asa Jewell and Henry C. Moses chosen Prudential Committee of Dist. 1.
17. Mrs. F—, aged 72, has knit 24 pairs of stockings this season for the soldiers.
18. The academical term closes and students gladly start for " Home, sweet home !" The friends of the Rev. Mr. Hoop-

MARCH, 1862.

er assemble at his house and present him about $100 in cash ; together with wood, flour, etc.

21. Rain, wind, snow and hail through the day, "Box" to S.Com.

23. Ther. 51. at 2 P. M. Lewis Oscar, son of Mrs. Jno. Leavitt, is severely injured in the head by a kicking horse.

24. Mr. Chas. F. Browne, alias "Artemas Ward," lectures at the Town Hall on the "Children in the Wood," to a small audience.

28. Mrs. Sarah G., wife of George Smith, Esq. dies, aged 71.

31. The ladies send a box of clothing, etc. to Co. B, Capt. Stanyon, 8th N. H. regt., at Ship Island, Miss. The News Letter commences its 32d volume.

APRIL—

1. The Maine 3d Battery passes through town.

4. Epigæa repens in bloom. Joseph T. Gilman, Esq. aged 50 years dies.

5. Snow in A. M. Travelling execrable. It has snowed 35 times during the winter, and we have had about 120 days of sleighing. Freese Dearborn, Esq. dies, aged 84 years and ten days. 7. Ther. 23. at 9 P. M.

8. Ther. 23. at 7 A. M. Wind N. W. Clear. Paraselene at 10 P. M. S. J. Court in session—Judge W. H. Bartlett. Orville P. Higgins, member of the senior class in Phillips Academy, dies at Portland, Me.

9. Rev. Charles Robinson, a native of Exeter, dies at Groton, Mass. aged 68 years.

10. Annual Fast. Sermon before the united churches, by Rev. E. Nason. Mr. Thomas E. Fifield, and Mrs. Mary N. Prescott are married, (at Lowell, Mass.)

12. Dea. Francis Grant crosses the river below the lower falls, upon the ice at noon. Day superb.

13. A very charming day. Hear the welcome song of the Phebe—[*Musicapa atra.*] 15. Bar. 30.49 at 9 P. M.

16. River clear of ice. Day warm and birds singing sweetly.

17. Ther. 74, at 2 P. M. Wind W.

18. Warm, sunny morning. Insects on the wing. Frogs are heard in the evening. " Box" sent to S. Com.

19. River full and flowing down over the upper dam like the long, golden, curling tresses of a young girl. Battle of South Mills, N. C. in which Capt. H. H. Pearson's Co. participates heroically without loss.

20. Dr. S. B. Swett is severely injured by being thrown from his gig. Mr. James Conden and Miss Jane Shimmick are married. Eggs are selling at 12 cts. per dozen ; ham at 10 cts. per lb.

21. An Aurora Borealis last night—a phenomenon quite infrequent this season.

APRIL, 1862.

22. Bar. 29.61 at 8 P. M. Mr. B. R. Downes, jr. gives a concert at the Town Hall.—Fee 15 cents.

24. Mr. Eben Folsom and Miss Hannah S. Bagley are married. S. S. Leavitt in town. Daniel McNary aged 16 years, killed on board the "Brooklyn," in the bombardment of Forts Phillips and Jackson.

25. The "Dido," latine rigged, arrives from Portsmouth. Messrs. Brown and bros. Hub Factory is in full operation. Abner Merrill, Esq. is chosen president of the Granite State Bank, vice Joseph T. Gilman, Esq., deceased.

26. Anemone nemorosa in bloom. Also, Prunus Americana.— Mrs. Henry Manjoy dies, aged 68. S. D. Lane, Esq. kills an ox which weighs 1600 lbs. when dressed.

27. Rev. Mr. Newhall lectures before the "Christian Fraternity."

28. Beautiful evening.—Robins sing till nearly 10 P. M. Sanguinaria canadensis in bloom.

30. Snow still lingers in shady places. Hear the Turdus felivox.—Robins incubating. Observe a very brilliant meteor like a rocket in the S. E. just after sunset. Hepatica triloba in bloom.

MAY—

1. Bar. 30.25 at 2 P. M. The ground is free from frost. Cold and chilly morning; a great many people out in quest of "May flowers." The Unitarian Society hold a very pleasant May Day Festival at the Town Hall. Tableaux and music in the evening very fine. The Sabbath School of the 1st Church make an excursion to the "Elysian Fields," in the afternoon.

5. Thunder storm at noon, and five elm trees on the Hampton road struck by lightning—also a white ash about 50 feet high, near Mr. Gilman Barker's, on the Brentwood road. Battle of Williamsburg. Va., in which the N. H. 2d regt., bravely participate, and in which, of this town, William H. Morrill is killed, Lieut. Albert M. Perkins, J F. Haines W. Floyd and G. H. Thing, wounded. Com. Long raises the "Stars and Stripes."

6. Bar. 29.50 at 2. P. M. Leontodon taraxicum in bloom.

7. Ther. 38. at 9 P. M. Hail storm at 2 P. M.

9. The Baltimore oriole—[*Icterus Baltimore*] appears.

10. Splendid golden clouds at sunset—fantastic forms—inter alia —a city with spires, pinnacles. etc., in gold, surrounded by dark masses of cumuli, from which five radiant purple bands shoot to the zenith. Also a volcanic mountain and the form of the "Monitor" with the prow directed south.

11. Blossoms of the red maple fall. Barn Swallows build their nests. The foam below the falls assumes peculiar geometrical figures. Butterflies appear. Houstonia cerulea in

MAY, 1862.

bloom. John S. Rock, Esq., (colored) lectures at the Town Hall

12. Bar. 30.25 at 7. A. M. The wild plum and strawberry are in bloom. The gladsome rigmarole of the bobolink [*D. orizyvorus*] is heard. Foam below the lower bridge assumes most beautiful and peculiar forms.

13. Probate Court in session. Judge Stickney presiding. Herring appear in the river. Currant—[*Ribes rubrum*] in blossom.

14. Erythronium americanum in bloom. Also the apple—very full. Ladies' Soldiers Aid Society hold their annual meeting. Mrs. E. Cobbs re-appointed president. Lt. A. M. Perkins arrives in town, wounded.

16. Our fresh water streams now teem with perch—[*perca flavescens*] pickerel, roach, ruffs, [*pomotis vulgaris*] with now and then a silver trout. Hear the sweet silvery song of the American nightingale—[*Turdus mustelinus.*] Farmers are planting corn and potatoes.

17. Ther. 86. at 2 P. M. Wind S. W.

18. Severe thunder storm from 3 to 4 P. M. White birch [*Betula populi-folia*] in bloom.

19. Thunderstorm and vivid lightning at 3 P. M.

20. Notice a glow worm, [*Lampyris*]—unusual here ; also a nighthaw [*caprimulgus virginianus*].

21. N. G. White, Esq. and Miss Mary Ann, daughter of the late Hon. James Bell, are married.

24. Lilac in perfect flower.

25. A slight frost last night, by which early plants were injured. Rev. Mr. Hooper lectures before the "Christ'n Fraternity."

27. Spring Beauty [*Claytonia Virginiana*] in bloom. Also Kalmia glauca [rare].

33. Vast numbers of chimney swallows assemble at night-fall ; wheel for half an hour or so with merry song around a chimney near and take up lodgings for the night. Front street now is beautiful as the grove of Academus.

30. Barberry, cornel and sorrel in bloom. Bees begin to swarm. Vibrations in the sheet of water rolling over the lower dam very distinct and beautiful. What causes them ?

JUNE—

1. Ilex opaca floret.

2. Miss A. C. Morris' Female Academy commences.

3. Sarracenia purpurea in bloom.

4. Rain all day. Mr. Knight D. Cheney and Miss Elizah D. daughter of the late Sam'l G. Smith, Esq., are married.

5. The morning, after the refreshing rain of yesterday, opens clear and inaugurates a most beautiful day.

6. The Academy now has 105 students; our High School 77.

2

June, 1862.

Mr. John F. Smith from Culpepper C. House, Va., arrives in town. Also, Mr. Colbath who was taken prisoner at Bull Run. The "Bell Ringers," give a concert at the Town Hall.

7. The fields are in "deepest verdure clad," and give promise of an abundant harvest. Rain at night. F. Tebbetts taken prisoner at Bull Run, arrives at New York.

8. Ther. 49. at 9 p. m.

9. Nature smiling in serenest beauty.—Serenading by the Student's Band in the evening. Mr. Jno. Maeder d. aged 86.

10. The depot of the B. and M. R. R. broken open last night, and robbed of about $10, in cents.—Mr. John Gilman's store also broken open. The thief caught. Locust-tree [*Robinia pseudacacia*] in bloom. Parties enjoying boat excursions up the river.

11. An eclipse of the moon. Total obscuration commences at 5 min. before 12 M., and continues one hour and 7 min.— A few light cirrus clouds cover the moon's disc. Wind S. W. An Aurora Borealis at the time.

12. Bar. 29.55 at 2 p. m.—Wind W.

13. Waterlily, [*nymphœa odorata*] in bloom, rare.

14. A slight frost occurred last night, by which some vines were injured. Several academy boys recruiting soldiers for the army. 15. The Rev. Dr. C. Francis preaches in town.

16. Bar. 30.29 at 9 p. m. Wind N. W. clear. Mr. Jacob Stone returns from Port Royal, S. C.—sick. Battle at James Island, S. C.—N. H. 3d regt. engaged and the following Exeter men wounded :—Wm. Caban, in the breast, mortally ; Samuel Caban, in the leg ; Jacob Smith, in the breast ; Wm. Marston, in the leg, and Daniel W. Elliott, in the arm.

17. Find wild strawberries ripe. Gardens now looking finely.

18. Forty five persons present at the union prayer meeting at 8 a. m. 19. Fire-flies abundant in the evening.

21. Hear the song of a robin as early as 3 o'clock this morning. Heavy shower in the evening.

22. The Rev. Mr. Tilden lectures to the "Christian Fraternity." Theme—Amos Lawrence.

23. Strawberries abundant ; large and of fine flavor.

24. The foliage of the currant and gooseberry bushes injured by worms peculiar to those shrubs.

25. Easterly winds high last night with rain. Clara G. dau. of Gideon and Abigail Carter, dies, aged 2 years and 10 mos. Mr. Charles P. Wright and Miss Martha J., daughter of Wm. H. Clarke, Esq. are married.

26. Green peas, brought from E. Kingston, are selling at 8 shillings per bushel.—Rainy day. Mr. C. C. Stevens is recruiting for the 9th regt.

June, 1862.

27. Mr. S. G. Pillsbury, student, leaves for Manchester with 25 recruits (5 students) for the 9th reg't. Farmers commence haying. Some use the mowing machine. Mr. J. B. Robinson, Co. C, 6th regt. dies at Roanoake Island, aged 40 years. Sweet brier in bloom.

28. Ther. 86. at 2 P. M. Wind W.—clear. Messrs. Carter brothers open a bath house on Water st. The canker worm has destroyed the foliage of some appletrees in this; and many, in neighboring towns. It disappeared the 20th inst.

29. Battle at Savage's Station. Augustus J. Leavitt, Mass. 29th reg taken prisoner. F. Tuck and E. Gill grad. at Dart. Coll.

30. Great excitement occasioned by reports of battles in front of Richmond, Va, in which our men engage.

July—

1. Bar. 29.61 at 7 A. M. A gloomy uncertainty in the minds of the people resp'g the fate of our army at Richmond

2. John T. Perry, Editor of the Cincinnati Gazette, in town.

3. Ther. 54. at 7 A M. Rain.—Wind E.

4. Bar. 30.35 at 7 A. M. and 2 P. M. Fair. The bells ring an. hour in the A. M. The Baptist Societies unite in a picnic at Gilman's grove, and the 2d Church holds a Strawberry festival at the Town Hall in the evening. The day passes quietly.

5. Mr. Oliver Pray, of the Mass. 26th regt., and formerly of this town dies at Ft. Jackson, Miss. aged about 50 years.

6. Ther. 91 1-2. at 2 P. M. Cherries and currants ripe and plentiful.

7. The ladies hold a preliminary meeting on behalf of our sick and wounded soldiers.

8. Examination at the Academy. Dr. Burroughs and other of the trustees present. Mr. Packard's Concert at the Town Hall is well attended—fee 25 cents.

9. Mr. Theodore R. Parker and Miss Eliza M. Cate are mar.

10. Levee at the Town Hall for raising money for the sick and wounded soldiers ;—large attendance.

12. Our High School closes. 13. Beautiful moonlight evening.

14. A war meeting is held at the Town Hall. Hon. Amos Tuck, chairman. Mr. W. Sanderson and Miss Carrie E. Piper are married.

15. A dull rainy day.—War news discouraging.

19. Miss Mary A., daughter of Mr. George W. Witherell, dies, aged 15 years and 11 mos. An infant daughter of J. Warren Towle Esq. dies. Mr. Wm. Dolloff dies, aged 77 yrs.

20. Silver change has almost entirely disappeared and glutinized postage stamps take the place of it.

23. The Cashier of the Granite State Bank receives two coun-

ULY, 1862.

terfeit one hundred dollar bills on the Merrimack Co.
Bank, Concord. The Portsmouth and Newmarket Banks
were also deceived.

25. An abundance of wild raspberries this season.

27. Clear and pleasant evening.

28. Ladies still toiling energetically on behalf of the soldiers.

AUGUST—

1. The town vote to pay a bounty of $100 to each recruit in a
new, and $125 to each recruit in an old, regiment.

2. Miss Elizabeth, eldest daughter of Mr. Thomas and Mary
Wainwright, dies, in her 17th year. Mr. Henry Wood,
Co. D, 4th N. H. regt. and Miss Caroline F. Weeks are
married.

6. James M. Lovering, Esq. is appointed Collector of Internal
Revenue for N. H. District No 1. A party of Exeter
young men establish Camp "Cobb," at Hampton Beach,
where many of our citizens are now recreating, C. P. H
Nason graduates at Williams, S. P. Dame at Bowdoin Coll

8. Ther. 84. at 2, P. M. 9. Bar. 29.65 at 2 P. M.

10. The dwelling house of Mr. Daniel S. Mace on the Epping
road destroyed by fire. Loss $700—$400 insured.

11. The President's call for 300,000 additional men is warmly
approved and many are enlisting. Remarkably fine sunset.

12. Coal is selling at $8.50 per ton.

13. A grand war meeting at the Town Hall. Addresses by
Messrs. Kidder, Wood, Nason, etc.

15. Lt. W. H. Smith ar. in town from Harrison's Landing, Va.

16. A comet visible a few degrees S. of the N. star—not well
defined. 17. Bar. 30.35 at 7 A. M.—Fair and cool.

18. Very fine "Northern Light," at 9 P. M. 30 deg. in altitude.

19. Many of our citizens are enjoying the sea-breeze at Hampton Beach. Silence of the evening broken by the "fife
and drum." 20. The Rev. Martin Moore in town.

21. The Maine 17th regt. passes through town in 17 cars.

23. A rainy and dull day. Frank A., son of Mr. Franklin
Rowe, dies at Chicopee, Mass, and is buried at Exeter,
aged 16 years 2 mos. and 5 days,

25. Bar. 30.35. at 9 P M. Rev. J. F. Whitney and Miss Vic-
toria Piper are married.

25. Schools commence in district No. 1. A. P. Blake, Esq. is
appointed Assistant U. S. Assessor for Exeter, North
Hampton, etc. A town meeting in reference to the war.
W. B. Morrill, Esq., moderator. Comet moving S. and
decreasing.—Tail dimly visible.

26. Ladies forward a box of Hospital stores to the "Sanitary
Commission." Mr. Theodore Moses, for many years a
resident of this town, dies at Newmarket, aged 95 yrs. and

AUGUST, 1862.

    11 months. Ho leaves 8 children, 28 grand children and about 30 great grand children.

27. Mrs Sarah, widow of the late Dea. Josiah Folsom, dies, aged 83 years.

28. Blueberries selling at 3 cts. per quart.—Hay crop very good. Golden rod [*solidago canadensis*] in bloom. Catharine Halion dies, aged 33. 23 volunteers leave for the war.

29. Bar. 29.65 at 7 A. M.—Weather fine. Battle of Bull Run, in which the 6th N. H. regt. is sharply engaged. Albert Bowley is wounded in the shoulder; S. S. Hodgdon in the hand; Morris Redding loses a thumb; Wm. and Jno. Doody, Wm. Ryan, A. J. Davis and Frank Corcoran are missing.—The N. H. 2d regt. lose in all 132 men in this engagement.

30. Cardinal Flower [*Lobelia cardinalis*] in bloom. The "army worm," does not appear this season.

31. Ther. 50. at 7 A. M. Battle of Bull Run continues. Miss Adaline H. daughter of Mr. Henry Burley dies aged 29 years and 6 mos.

SEPTEMBER—

1. Rainy. Ladies send a box of hospital stores to the Sanitary Commission. From Sept. 1861 to Sept. 1862, Mrs. W. has knit 50 pairs of stockings for the soldiers.

2. Bar. 29.50 at 7 A. M. Lovely day. A slight frost observed this A. M. in low grounds. Charles Edwin, son of Stephen J. and Ellen M. Dudley dies, aged 1 year and 11 mos.

3. Sad tidings from the seat of war. Mr. Frank L. Tibbetts and Miss Mary Jane Purinton (of Epping) are married.

4. Splendid weather. The quota of soldiers from Exeter is already made up. The friends of Maj. M. N. Collins, N. H. regt. present him a sword, belt, sash, etc., on his departure for the war. Many of our people attend the Camp Meeting at Newmarket Junction.

5. Another "box" sent by our patriotic ladies to the soldiers.

6. Ther. 84. at 2 P. M.—Wind W.

7. Wind E. Cloudy in the A. M. Fair in the P. M. An eagle is seen perched for some time on the hand of the statue of Justice, surmounting the dome of the Court House.

9. Charming day. Great anxiety for the safety of Washington.

12. About 40 men under Capt. Julian leave for the war. The academy has 125 pupils.

14. Bar. 30.40 at 7 A. M. N. H. 11th regt., containing several Exeter men, arrives at Washington, D. C. Mr. Frank E. Dearborn and Miss Carrie S. Batchelder are married Also, Mr. Charles E. Young and Miss Olivia A. Wiggin.

16. The leaves of the birch, maple, etc. begin to change color.

18. The great battle of Antietam, in which the N. H. 5th, 6th,

2*

SEPTEMBER, 1862.

and 9th regts. are engaged. B. Wadleigh, M. D. French, and Samuel Page are wounded.

18. Bartlett Pears are selling at $1 per bushel.

19. John Marshall, son of Mrs. E. Cobb, 1st mate of the "Sea King," is lost with that vessel, 10 days out from San Francisco to Liverpool.

24. A "box" sent to the S. Commission by the ladies.

25. An officer recruiting for the navy hangs his flag out at the Squamscott. Beautiful Aurora Borealis at 9 P. M.—radiant.

26. Ther. 44. at 7 A. M. A heavy frost last night. Mr. Wm. T. Bradwick and Miss Jennie R. James are married.— Also, Lt. Wm. H. Sythes and Miss Asenath Haughey.

27. Rainy. Rev. Mr. Lanphear lectures to the "Christian Fraternity."

30. Apples abundant and selling at $1 per bbl. Cider the same.

OCTOBER—

1. A rainy day. Dr. Wm. Perry is appointed to examine such enrolled men as claim exemption from military duty.

2. Mr. N. M. Jewell is appointed U. S. Deputy Collector for Rockingham and Strafford Counties. A box of hospital stores forwarded by the ladies to the "S. Commission."

4. Appletrees are bending beneath their load of fruit, which is very fair and large. I count forty carriages and teams in Water st.

6. Prof. Henry B. Nason in town—also, Ex-president Franklin Pierce, who has been spending some time at Little Boar's Head. 7. Col. W. G. Veazie in town.

8. Ther. 85. at 2 P. M. A charming day. U. S. District Court in session. Judge Harvey presiding.

9. Ther. 85 at 2 P. M. Dr. John Sullivan, Jr. arrives in town from Paducah, Ky. Mr. Charles E. Hall, Master of Transportation of the B. and M. R. R., and formerly of Exeter, dies, aged 44 years.

10. The Commissioner of Pensions has appointed Dr. Wm. G. Perry an examining surgeon.

11. Five dogs are poisoned by strychnine, in Franklin street.

12. The Rev. Chas. Beecher preaches at the Lower Church.

13. Rainy. 14. Archelaus B. Huso dies, aged 30 yrs. & 9 mos.

15. Mr. Josiah Dearborn, formerly of this town, dies in Methuen, Mass., about this time, aged 56 years.

16. The 25th Maine regt. Col. F. Fessenden, passes through town. Messrs. G. C. Lyford, & Co. issue "Scrip," redeemable at the Granite State Bank. 17. Cloudy and cold.

18. Wind W.—fair. Grapes abundant.

19. Pick ripe raspberries in an open field.

OCTOBER, 1862.

20. Exeter soldiers in the Washington hospitals ; W. Ryan shot in the side ; P. W. Sullivan ; Jno. Doody wounded in the hip ; Stephen White. Mr. Chas. Wm. Young leaves for Concord, with 17 recruits. The foliage of the forest less beautifully tinted than in October last.

21. First heavy frost of the season. Ther. 28. at 7. A. M.

22. Bar. 40 at 2 P. M.

23. Thomas R. Davis, Esq. and Miss Lydia A. Flagg are mar.

24. Bar. 30.45 at 7. A. M. Ther. 24. Water froze last night. Cotton sheetings sell at 25 cts. pr yard. George Albert, son of Albert S. and Mary J. Smith, dies, aged 4 yrs. and 2 mos.

25. Miss Margaret Emery dies, aged 90 yrs. and 10 days. The Barker Family give a concert in the Town Hall.

27. Bar. 29.40 at 2 P. M. Heavy rain last night with easterly winds. Trees partially bereft of foliage.

28. Rev. Mr. Hadley, of Portland, holds a meeting in the Town Hall, on behalf of the Sanitary Commission.

29. James M. Tappan, Student, Co. A, 9th regt., dies at Pleasant Valley, Md., aged 29 years and 8 mos.

30. Mr. Samuel Tilton, formerly of this town, is erecting an elegant mansion on Beacon St., Boston.

31. Mr. Augustus Weeks' family came near being suffocated by kerosene oil left burning in the night.

NOVEMBER—

1. Ther. 64. at 2 P. M. Clear, wind W. "Indian Summer."

2. Mr. Jno. Wm. Coffin and Miss Sarah A. Brown are mar.

3. Windy and warm in the morning ; cold and clear in the evening. " The dead leaves strew the forest walk."

5. Thirty-five persons present at the morning prayer meeting. Mr. John Dolloff dies at Jacksonville, aged 24 yrs. 6 mos.

7. First snow storm of the season commences at 11 A. M.–severe.

9. Bar. 29.50 at 2 P. M. An extremely disagreeable day. Mr. Gilman Smith gathers a bunch of ripe strawberries in his garden, and sends them to Boston.

10. Wild geese are moving over the town toward the " sunny south." 12. Mr. George Daniels dies, aged about 60 yrs.

13. Our ladies—zealous in every good work—send a "box," containing 399 articles to the S. Commission. Mr. John L. Dearborn and Miss Sarah A. Abbot, daughter of the late Samuel G. Smith, Esq., are married.

15. Maj. G. Carlton Smart dies—suddenly—aged 87 yrs. 5 mo.

16. Bar. 30.91 at 7 A. M. [maximum for the year] 30.88 at 2 P. M. 30.85 at 9 A. M.—Wind N. at 7 A. M. and clear.— William Cole, Esq., and Miss Susan L. Page, are married at Hampton. Corn meal $1.75 per bag.

17. Hon. John Sullivan, son of Hon. George Sullivan, dies sud-

NOVEMBER, 1862.

denly, aged 62 years. Mr. Charles H. Goodwin issues scrip of small denominations.

18. This day opens splendidly—and closes clear, serene and beautiful. Inveni diem.

19. Rainy day. A number of our teachers attend the meeting of the N. H. Association of teachers at Nashua.

20. Rain storm continues. Kerosene oil selling at $1.00 per gall. Hard wood $6.00 per cord.

21. Ther. 5. at 7 A. M. Storm continues—warm and dark.

22. Mrs. Persis, widow of the late John Bell, dies at Chester, aged 84 years. The rain storm which began on the 19th inst. closes to-night. John H. Carpenter, 8th regt. dies ab. this time at N. Orleans. 23. Fair and cold.

26. Examination at the Academy.—Dr. A. P. Peabody and other literati present. The Young Ladies' High School, under Miss Morris, closes. Chanc'r Joseph Gibson Hoyt, L. L. D. formerly of Exeter, dies at St. Louis, aged 48.

27 ANNUAL THANKSGIVING.—Sermon to the united churches by the Rev. Mr. Hooper.

28. John T. Perry. Esq., Editor of the Cincinnati Gazette, and Miss Sarah N. Chandler of Concord, are married.

29. Very little sickness in town.

30. Mrs. Ruth Stevenson, wife of Mr. E. S. Durgin, dies, aged 48 years and 7. mos. We have three snows which cover the ground this month.

DECEMBER—

1. Our traders have entered into an agreement to close their stores at 8 o'clock P. M. Schools begin in Dist. Nos. 1 & 2.

2. Prof. J. G. Hoyt is buried from the 2d Church. The Cotton Factory is, after a long time, started.

6. Bar. 29.10 at 7 A. M. About 8 inches of snow fell last night.—The forests covered with the fleecy burden present a very beautiful and unique appearance. Sleighing commences. Miss Jane Atherton dies of consumption, aged 23 years.

9. Ther. —3. at 7 A. M. Charles O. Brown, Esq. and Miss Sarah B. Piper are married. 10. Ther. 56. at 2 P. M.

11. Weather fine. Academical term commences.

13. Rain and Snow. Great Battle at Fredericksburg, Va — Many N. H. regts. engaged. James M. Sleeper killed; Richard Neally, Newton Cram, Freeman Conner, and Leonard H. Caldwell, [of the academy,] wounded—the latter mortally.

14. News of the defeat of Burnside's army at Fredericksburg, saddens every heart.

1771724

DECEMBER, 1862.

15. A " box " sent by our ladies to the S. Commission.

20. Very cold day—average temperature —1.3°.

21. Bar. 30.96 at 2 P. M.   Ther. attached 66.

24. The Unitarian Society have a pleasant Christmas Festival.

25. " Merrie Christmas."   The 2d Church hold a levee at the Town Hall.

26. Rainy and warm.   A valuable " box," forwarded to the S. Commission, containing—inter alia—eight one gallon jars of jelly.   About $450 in cash have been expended in filling the boxes for the soldiers this year.

Our 2, 5, 6, 9, 10, 11 & 12 Regiments are at Falmouth, Va.—Our 3 & 4 are at Hilton Head—and our 8th is at New Orleans.

31. Dull cold day.   The Rev. Mr. Hooper's society has a very pleasant festival at the T. Hall.   Mr. D. S. Mace and Miss M. J. Fellowes are married.

So ends a year of rebellion, trial, toil and bloodshed,—of exalted patriotism and loyalty, as of national agony : but HOPE leaning on the arm of HIM who defends the right and controls the destinies of the nations, sends her brightening eye into the year now opening, and beholds the Rainbow of peace serenely smiling on the bosom of the storm.

NAMES

OF

EXETER SOLDIERS.

ENLISTED IN 1861-62.

Abbott, S. T. 8, B.
Allard, Job C. 13. E.
Avery, Alfred A. 9, A.
Barker, J. J. D. 11, I.
Bean, Wm. 6, C.
Batchelder, Geo. 15, I.
Batchelder, C. W. 9, A.
Bearse, Frederick 11, I.
Bennett, Edw. T. 6, C, dis.
Benrett, Jno. H 2, E.
Bennett, Chas. 7, Me.
Berry, Woodbury, 3, B.
Bowley, Albert 6, C, dis. w.
Bowley, Benj. F. 6, C, dis.
Brigham, Aziel P. 15.
Brigham, Geo. H. U. S. N.
Brigham, Eph. 15.
Brigham, W. H. Bruce 15.
Broderick, Wm. U. S. N.
Broadbent, Jno. 3, B.
Brown, Jno. C. 13, E.
Brown, G. W. R. I. Cav.
Brown, Geo. H. 14, Mass.
Bryant, Jno. S. 3, C.
Caban, Freeman U. S. N.
Caban, Samuel 3, B, w. dis.
Cabun, Wm. 3, B, killed.
Caldwell, L. H. 9, A, Sergt, w.
Caldwell, Frank M. 9, A, sergt.
Carter, Gideon 15, I.
Carter, F. W. 15, I.
Carpenter, Jno. H. 8, B, d.
Carnece, James 3, B.
Carter, Gideon, Jr., 3, B.
Carter, W. Edwin 15, I.
Carver, E. 8, B.
Caswell, Jno. K. 9, D.

Chase, Wm. U. S. N.
Chase, Jas. W. 2, E.
Cilley, J. K. 11, Lt.
Clark, Wm. A. 12, Mass., Corp.
Clark, Geo. W. 14 Mass., Sergt.
Clement, J. W. 3, B.
Clough, George 3, B.
Clough, Thomas H. 6, C, dis.
Clough, Ezekiel " "
Cobbs, George S. 8, B, Sergt.
Cokely, T. 8, B.
Colbath, Charles W. 3, B.
Colcord, Charles, E. 2. E, dis.
Colcord, William H. " "
Collins, M. N. 11, Lt. Col.
Conner, Freeman 44.N.Y.,Col.,w.
Conner, E. J. 17, reg. U.S.A. Capt.
Conner, John U. S. N.
Corcoran, Frank 6, C.
Cotter, Maurice 9, Mass., d.
Cram, Alanson 11, I.
Cram, Newton, 13, E,w.
Crane Patrick 9, A.
Cummings, Dr. E. P. U. S. N.
Currier, Andrew J. 2, E.
Curtis A. O. 13, Mass., d.
Davis, A. J. 6, C.
Davis C. H. B, 3.
Dearborn, Calvin L. 3, E, d.
Dearborn, A. 4.
Dearborn, Geo. 15. Mass. Batt'y.
Dearborn, W. S. 3, B.
Dearborn, J. S. Cook's Mass. Battery, dis.
Dearborn, J. F. 9, A.
Dewhurst, G.W. Act'g Mat'r,U.S. N
Dewhurst, George W. Adj.

Dolioff, J. L, 13, E.
Donnavan C. 3, B.
Donnavan, J. 8, B.
Doody, Jno. 6, C. w.
Doody, Wm. " "
Dodge J. E. 22 Mass., Q.M. Serg't.
Dudley, S. G., 3, B.
Dudley, D. W. 3, B.
Duffee, Jno. 3, B, d.
Durgin, V. W. 8, B, corp.
Durgin, Wm. E. 14. Me., K.
Dyer, John, Jr., 8, B.
Elkins, James 6, C. dis.
Elliott, D. W. 3, B.
Ellison, Frank, 2, E.
Ellison, Horace, 5, Mass., dis.
Farnham, Jno. 5, Mass.
Farnham, Jas. M. 6, C.
Fielding, J. 3, B.
Finn, Jno. 3, B.
Floyd, C. W. 2, E. w. [at Will'g]
Floyd, Samuel 2, discharged.
Fogg, Andrew J. Lt., 3, B.
Furnald, J. F 4.
Foss, Chas. H. 8, B.
Folsom, Jos. 13,
Folsom, C. E. 17, Mass.
Foster, F. H. 9, A.
French, M. D. 9, A, dis. w.
Fuller, George W. 13, E.
Gale, G. W. Jr., Assist. Sur. U.S.N.
Gadd, G. W. 15, I.
Garland, Geo. E. 13. E.
Gasand, Jas. H. 14, Mass., d.
Giddings, Geo. H. 3, B, corporal.
Gill, Is. W. Act'g Master, U. S. N.
Gill, Nathaniel 11, Mass., mus'n.
Gill, Geo. R. I. Cavalry.
Gilman, A. J. 13, E.
Gilman, J. W. 11, I.
Gilman, Gardner 45, Mass.
Gilman, Geo. 8, B.
Goodwin, Thos. 9, A.
Goodwin, Sewell U. S. N., w.
Gordon, Jno. 25, Mass., corporal.
Greenleaf, M. N. 6, C, Lt.
Greenleaf, Chas. 15, I.
Hale, Charles E. 8, B, fifer, dis.
Hale. John H. 2, E, dis.
Haines Daniel D. 8, B, corp.
Haines. Isaiah F. 2, E, w.
Hall, Edward F. 3, B.
Hall, Horace J 3, B.
Hartnett, Daniel P. 3, B.
Hartnett, J. H. 2, E.
Hartnett, Michael U. S. N.

Hartnett, Thomas 6, C.
Harris, D. D. 8, B.
Head, J. M. 3, D, Lt.
Head, O. M. 8, Adj.
Healey Ira 8, B.
Hervey, Frank H. 2, E.
Hibberd, Erskine W. 3, clerk, dis.
Hodgdon, S S. 6, C, w.
Huse, J. H. 2, E.
James, Geo. R. 3, D.
Janvrin, G. N. Cobb's Battery.
Janvrin, J. E 16, Assist. Surg.
Julian G. A. 13, E, Capt,
Keefe, Wm. 6, C.
Keyes, Philander 9, A.
Kelly, D. G. 8, B.
Kimball, G. N. U. S. N., dis.
Kincade, James U. S. N.
Lamprey, S. 3, B, Lt.
Lamson, Rufus 13, E.
Leavitt, E. A. 2, E, dis.
Leavitt, C. H. 29, Mass.
Leavitt, A. J. 29, Mass., dis.
Leavitt, J. W. 5, Mass., V. M.
Leavitt, Jno, 13, E.
Leavitt, W. R. 3, B, d.
Leighton, J. A. 6, C Serg't., dis.
Little, Patrick 9, A.
Lord, J. G. 9, A.
Lovering, E. E. 6, C.
Manjoy, Jno. U. S. N.
MARSTON, GILMAN, BRIG. Gen.
Marston, W. S. 3, B, w.
Marsh, A. F. 6, C, d.
M'Kusick, E. 9, A, Sergt.
M'Nary, Daniel U. S. N., k.
M'Nary, Thos. 8, B.
M'Neal, 19, Mass.
Melvin, M. 8, B
Merrill, A. 12, Mass., E.
Morrill, W. H. 2, E, k.
Morse, J. W. 15, I.
Morrison, Wm J. 3, B.
Moses, H. M. 13, E.
Murphy, J. 8, B.
Murphy, Dennis 2, E.
Nason, P. F., Q. M. Martin's Brig.
    Battery.
Nealey, Charles H. 11, I.
Nealey, B. U. S. N.
Nealey, Richard 11, I, Sergt. w.
Nudd, William 15, I.
O'Bryan, Jno. U. S. N.
Odion, Dr. G. G. 19, Indiana.
Page, Charles 2, E.
Parker, J. J. D. 11, I.

Payson, T. H. 24, Mass. D. Major.
Payson, J. C. 13, Mass., Commissary Department.
PEARSON, H H. 6, Lt. Col. w.
Perkins, A. M. 2, Lt., w.
Perkins, Asa E. 40, N. Y., d.
Pettigrew, Francis 2. E.
Pickering, V. A. 2, Mass., k.
Pillsbury, S. H. 9, A, Capt.
Pike D. 2, E.
Prescott, J. E. 2, E.
Prescott, George A. 15, I.
Reardon, M. 6, C.
Reynolds, George H. 11, I.
Riley, Jno. Jr., 3, B.
Robinson, Wm. Jr., 2. E.
Robinson, Geo. W. 2S, Mass.
Robinson, Josiah B. 6, C, d.
Rock, J, 6, C, dis.
Rollins, George F. 13, E.
Rollins, Henry S. R, U. S. N.
Rowell, J. 6, C, Sergt.
Rundlett, F. G. U. S. N,
Rundlett, James 2, E.
Ryan, William 6, C.
Sanborn, A. J. 9, A.
Sawyer, F. W. 13, C.
Senior, W. 3, B.
Sinclair, J. T. 15, E.
Sinclair, J. E. 15, E.
Simons, C. J. 9, A, Sergt.
Sleeper, W. H 3, B.
Smith, Jeremiah W. 15, E.
Smith, M. M. 6, C.
Smith, G. H. " "
Smith, W. H. 3, E, Lieut.
Smith, Charles 2, Clerk, dis.
Smith, J. 3, B.
Smith, J. R. 44, Mass.
Stacy, —— U. S. N.
Staples, Christopher 9, A.
Staples, C. H. U. S. N., dis.
Stevens, George W. 6, C.
Stevens, Chester, 9, D, Capt.
Stickney, D. S. B.
Stickney, M. H. 11, I.
Stockman, F. 6, C.
Stone, D. W. U. S. N.
Stone, J. D. 3, B, dis.
Sullivan, Jno. 13, Assistant Surg.
Sullivan, P. W. 6, C.
Swain, G. W. " " dis.
Swasey, W. E. U. S. N.
Tanner, Jeremiah 2. E.
Tanner, Seth 9, A, dis.

Tanner, George W. 9, A.
Tappan, James M. 9, A, d.
Taylor, Josiah W. 11, I.
Taylor, G. A. 2, E, dis.
Tebbetts, J. 8, B.
Tebbetts, F. L. 2, E.
Tebbetts, J. I. U. S. N., dis.
Tebbetts, W. V. B. 17, Mass.
Thing, Frederick F. 13, E.
Thing, G. E. 8, B, dis.
Thing, J H 3, B, Sergt.
Thing, G H 2, E, w.
Thurston, J O 2. E.
Thurston, George K 15, I.
Thurston, Eugene 9, A.
Tilton, J G 8, B.
Tilton, William P 11. I.
Towle, Charles J, U S N.
Tuttle, James S 15, I.
Twilight, W H 1st Art'y, Mass.
Vanduzee, J H 13, E, Sergt.
Vanduzee, J C 13. E, Sergt.
VEAZEY, W G 15, Vt, Col,
Veazey, Henry
Vinal, G A W 6, Mass,, K.
Wadleigh, Jas. P 9, A, w.
Walton, W H 3, B,
Walker, H 8, B.
Watson, J M 3. B. Corp.
Wainwright, W. U S N.
Warren, E. U S N.
Weeks, H 6, C.
Weeks, John S 9, A.
Weeks, J E G 9, A.
Weeks, Nathaniel 2, U S N.
Weeks, H A 26, Mass.
Weeks, Jeremiah S 3, B.
Weeks, Joshua W Jr, 6, C.
West, William 13, E.
White, Woodbury C S, B.
White, S 6, C.,
Whitehouse, W
Wilbur, J E 3, B, Capt.
Willey, Alfred 17, U S A, dis.
Willey, Henry 17, U S A D.
Willey, Edwin Regt Mass.
Willey, James 13. Mass.
Willey, George U S N, k.
Willey, Charles N H Cavalry.
Wood, Henry 9, A.
Wyman, W 4.
Young, J R S, B.
Young, C W 2, 6, B.
Young, L H 13, E.
Total, - - - - 293

www.ingramcontent.com/pod-product-compliance
Lightning Source LLC
Chambersburg PA
CBHW021522270326
41930CB00008B/1051